BEANS TO CHOCOLATE

Sarah Ridley

Published in Canada
Crabtree Publishing
616 Welland Avenue
St. Catharines, ON
L2M 5V6

Published in the United States
Crabtree Publishing
PMB 59051
350 Fifth Ave, 59th Floor
New York, NY 10118

Published in 2019 by Crabtree Publishing Company

First Published in Great Britain in 2018 by Wayland

The Author and Publisher would like to thank Divine Chocolate and Trading Visions for their help with this book.

Author: Sarah Ridley

Editors: Sarah Peutrill, Petrice Custance

Design: Matt Lilly

Proofreader: Ellen Rodger

Prepress technician: Margaret Amy Salter

Print coordinator: Katharine Berti

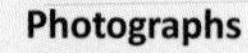

Photographs

Olivier Asselin/Divine Chocolate: 8. bigacis/Shutterstock: 17. Bloomberg/ Getty Images: 18. Bon Appetit/Alamy: 16br. Divine Chocolate: front cover b, 1b, 3t, 4, 5tl, 6, 7, 9b, 10, 12b, 14, 15, 20, 21, 22, 23, 24l. Food for Thought/ Alamy: 19b. Kim Naylor/Divine Chocolate: 9t, 11, 12t, 13, 24r. Julian Nieman/ Alamy: 16l. sursad/Shutterstock: 2, 5r. Norbert-Zsolt Suto/Alamy: 19t. Diana Taliun/Shutterstock: 3b. Tristan Tan/Shutterstock: front cover t, 1t.

Printed in the U.S.A./082018/CG20180601

Library and Archives Canada Cataloguing in Publication

Ridley, Sarah, 1963-, author
Beans to chocolate / Sarah Ridley.

(Where food comes from)
Includes index.
Issued in print and electronic formats.
ISBN 978-0-7787-5118-2 (hardcover).--
ISBN 978-0-7787-5129-8 (softcover).--
ISBN 978-1-4271-2166-0 (HTML)

1. Chocolate processing--Juvenile literature. 2. Cocoa processing--Juvenile literature. 3. Chocolate--Juvenile literature. I. Title.

TP640.R535 2018 j664'.5 C2018-902469-0
C2018-902470-4

Library of Congress Cataloging-in-Publication Data

CIP available at the Library of Congress

CONTENTS

Do you like chocolate? Chocolate is a food that many of us enjoy. The most important ingredient in chocolate is cocoa. But where does cocoa come from?

WHAT IS COCOA?

Cocoa is made from cocoa beans. Cocoa beans grow in pods on cocoa trees. Cocoa trees grow in countries near the **equator**, where the weather is hot and it rains often.

It all starts when farmers plant cocoa seeds.

Cocoa seeds grow into seedlings.

The seedlings then grow into cocoa trees.

COCOA FACT

Farmers **harvest** cocoa pods twice a year. Each time, they collect about 50 pods per tree.

COCOA TREES

Farmers care for the young cocoa trees. The trees flower when they are about four years old. The small flowers grow out of the cocoa tree's trunk or branches.

COCOA FACT

Insects crawl inside the flowers on cocoa trees to feed on **nectar**. The insects get covered in **pollen** and then pass the pollen on to other flowers. This is called **pollination**.

Each cocoa tree grows about 10,000 flowers a year. The flowers are difficult for insects to get inside, so only a few flowers on cocoa trees get pollinated. This is how the flowers make cocoa pods.

The cocoa farmers shown in this book belong to a **cooperative** called Kuapa Kokoo. It is located in Ghana, in West Africa.

COCOA FACT

As they **ripen**, cocoa pods change color, from green to yellow or orange.

To reach pods on high branches, farmers use a sharp knife on a long stick.

The Kuapa Kokoo farmers collect the cocoa pods and take them back to their village.

COCOA BEANS

The farmers split open the pods and empty the cocoa beans and slimy pulp into baskets.

There are about 40 cocoa beans inside each pod.

Next, the farmers spread the beans out on huge banana leaves. They cover the beans with more banana leaves. Everything is left to ferment for about one week.

WONDER WORD: FERMENT

When the beans ferment, tiny **fungi** called yeast start to break them down, changing how they taste.

This is what fermented cocoa beans look like.

The Kuapa Kokoo farmers spread the beans out on drying tables.

It takes up to 10 days for the cocoa beans to dry out in the sunshine. When the beans are dry, the farmers pack the beans into sacks.

COCOA FACT

It takes about 10 cocoa beans to make one small bar of milk chocolate.

Each sack of cocoa beans is weighed and tested for **quality**.

The Kuapa Kokoo farmers are paid a fair price for their cocoa beans by the **Ghana Cocoa Board**.

WONDER WORDS:
FAIR PRICE

A fair price is a payment that gives farmers and their families enough money to live on.

The Ghana Cocoa Board sells the cocoa beans to chocolate factories. The sacks of beans leave the Kuapa Kokoo farmers' village by truck.

MAKING CHOCOLATE

The sacks of cocoa beans travel by boat to chocolate factories around the world. When the beans arrive at the factories, they are sorted, cleaned, and roasted.

INSIDE THE ROASTER

After roasting, rollers crush the beans while another machine blows away the shells to leave cocoa nibs.

COCOA FACT

People who lived in South and Central America about 2,500 years ago used cocoa beans to make a frothy, bitter drink.

Another machine grinds the cocoa nibs into a paste. The paste is melted to make a liquid called cocoa liquor.

COCOA LIQUOR

Some of the cocoa liquor is pressed to separate it into cocoa powder and yellow cocoa butter.

COCOA BUTTER

To make milk chocolate, workers add some cocoa butter, milk, and sugar to the cocoa liquor.

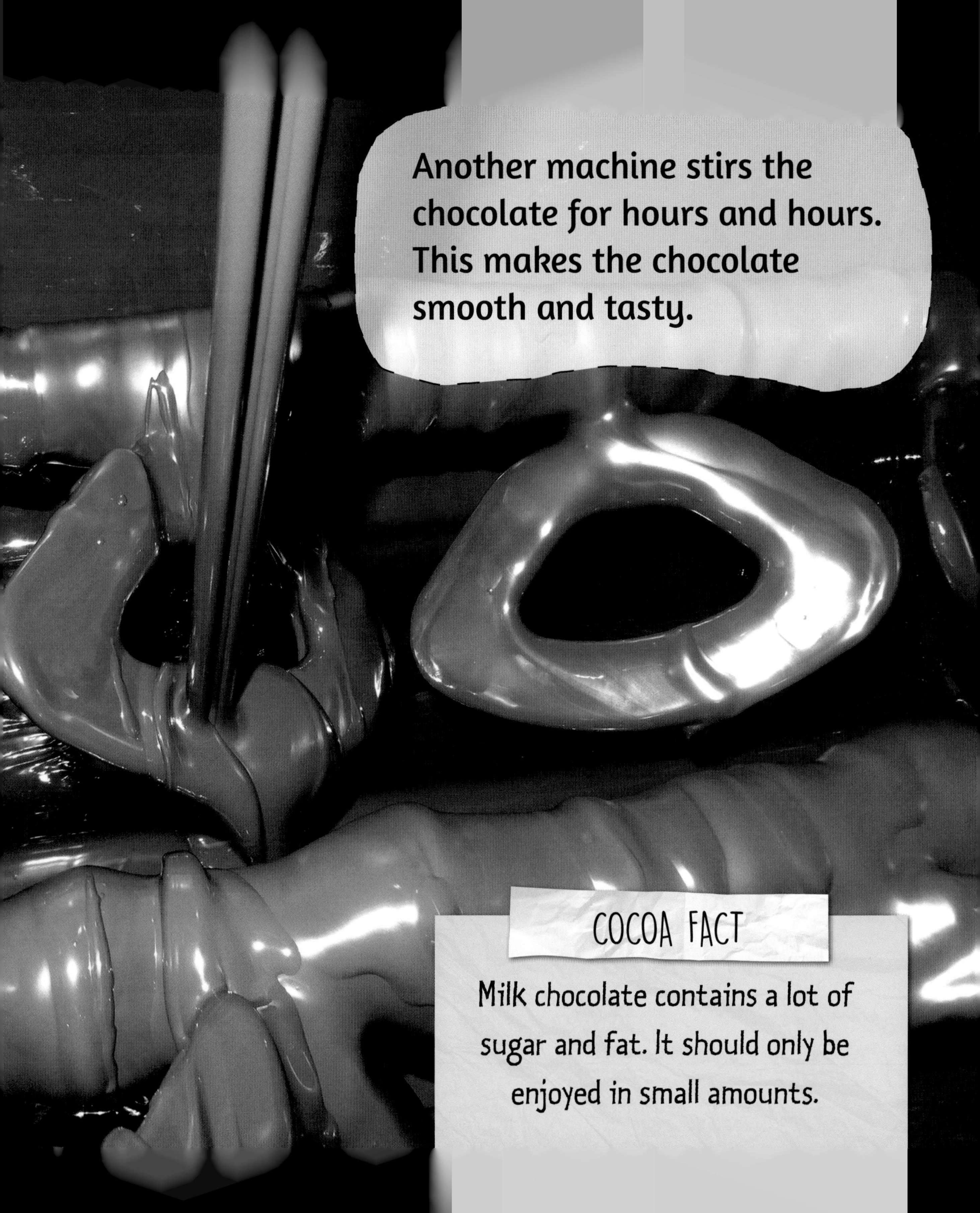

Another machine stirs the chocolate for hours and hours. This makes the chocolate smooth and tasty.

COCOA FACT

Milk chocolate contains a lot of sugar and fat. It should only be enjoyed in small amounts.

The chocolate is then poured into molds.

When cool, the chocolate bars are tipped out of the molds, packaged, and shipped to stores.

FAIRTRADE CHOCOLATE

When you buy chocolate, look for the Fairtrade logo on the packaging. This means that the cocoa farmers were paid a fair price for their cocoa beans. It also means they had good **working conditions.**

When farmers receive a fair price for their work, it helps to improve many lives. The Kuapa Kokoo farmers were able to buy a new water pump for their village.

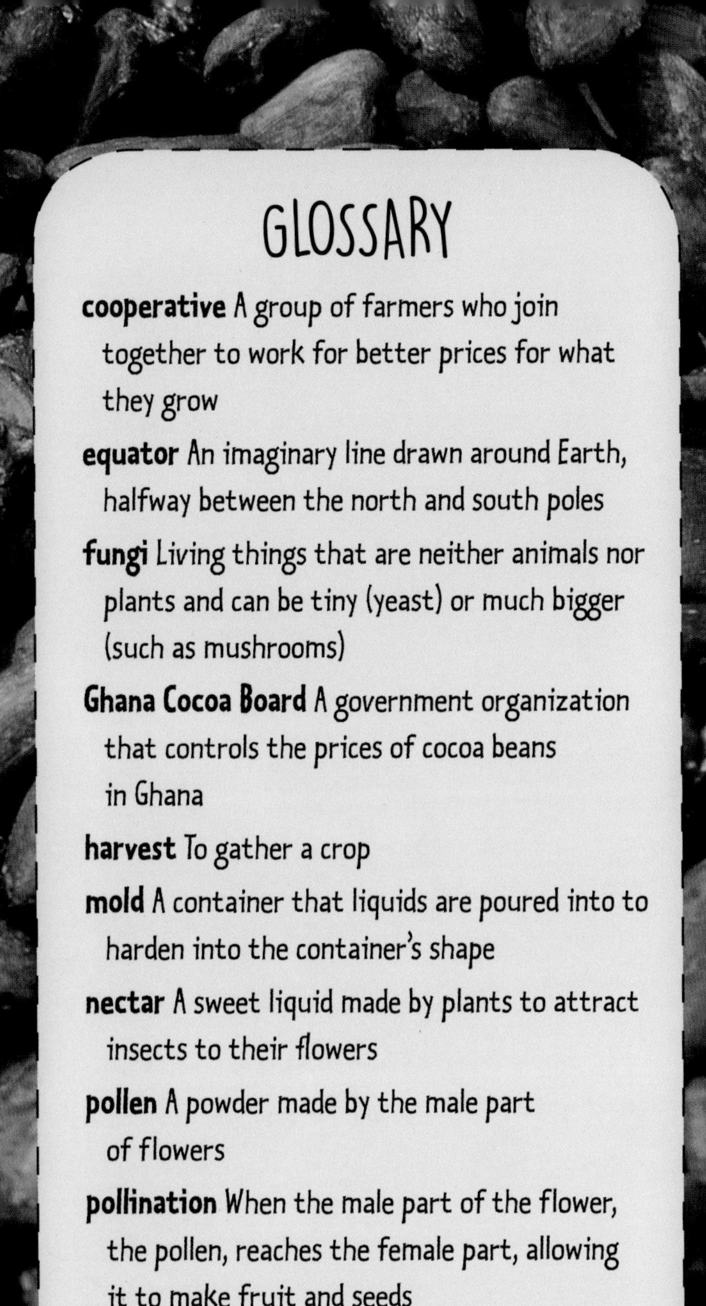

GLOSSARY

cooperative A group of farmers who join together to work for better prices for what they grow

equator An imaginary line drawn around Earth, halfway between the north and south poles

fungi Living things that are neither animals nor plants and can be tiny (yeast) or much bigger (such as mushrooms)

Ghana Cocoa Board A government organization that controls the prices of cocoa beans in Ghana

harvest To gather a crop

mold A container that liquids are poured into to harden into the container's shape

nectar A sweet liquid made by plants to attract insects to their flowers

pollen A powder made by the male part of flowers

pollination When the male part of the flower, the pollen, reaches the female part, allowing it to make fruit and seeds

quality A level of excellence

ripen To become ready to eat

working conditions The treatment and surroundings an employee experiences while working

INDEX